ACCOUNTABILITY

SHOW UP AND WIN

BY JON ROBERT QUINN

Page 3 | Introduction

Page 6 | Winner's Mentality

Page 13 | Time Management

Page 19 | Show Up

Page 21 | A Better You

Page 32 | Quit Making Excuses

Page 44 | Setting Goals

Page 48 | The Extra Mile

Page 53 | Setting Expectations

Page 60 | Success Isn't Luck

Page 64 | Dream Big

Page 70 | Fear with Cripple You

Page 76 | Conclusion

ACCOUNTABILITY

Introduction

This book was a long time coming. For years now, friends, family and colleagues have asked me how I continue to win not realising that I have the same daily struggles as them. I think the difference is that I just keep my head down and stay the course. My career has not always been filled with wins. In fact, I have had more losses than wins if you want my honest opinion. I fail every single day in one way or another. And yet, my peers think that money just falls from the sky into my lap. Most of them probably have more money than I do, I just allocate my money in areas that are construction rather than destructive.

ACCOUNTABILITY

Maybe I have a different philosophy than most. Maybe I am more calculated. Maybe God gave me a bunch of talents and the course to use those talents to make a lasting impression on the world. I honestly don't know. I just wake up every day and follow my heart and speak up when I see something that needs said.

I have always been a talker. When I was in school, I would do more talking than listening. I was cocky and thought my shit didn't stink. I think it was part of a defence mechanism to protect myself from all the abuse I got at home as a kid. I have always been observant and dissected everything I saw and heard. Why did they say that? Why did they do that? I learned early on to see patterns in behaviour. I read people like a book.

In one of my books I talked about listening to story people tell rather than listening to their words. People are pretty much full of shit, all the time. All of them are. Arrogance does most of our talking in society. We have to listen through the garbage and find the true meanings of their words. Once you learn this skill you will be able to identify who you can and cannot trust.

This book will be an eye opener for you. I want you to take what I am saying in this book and listen to the story I'm telling, rather than the words. There are lessons here. Apply these lessons. Half of winning is just showing up. I know that sounds facetious, but as you get through this book, I truly believe it will all start to make sense. Apply these lessons and I am positive you will see improvement in your daily life.

ACCOUNTABILITY

Winner's Mentality

In my introduction, I talked about how so many people think I'm always wining. Technically, I do win. But in reality, I have wins and losses like everybody else. Let's dissect what a win and loss are.

When you set a goal and you hit that goal, it's a win right? Well, sure. You had a vision of where you wanted to go. You figured out a course of action. Then, you did the necessary steps in order to accomplish those goals. Sounds like a win to me. Well, what about if you missed your goal. Would that be a loss? Well, sure. If you had your heart set on meeting those expectations or meeting that accomplishment and you failed to complete the task, you could look at it as a loss. But, you also won.

You gained a lot of experience and knowledge in "failing" to meet that goal. You took an honest effort and changed your path. It may have been change of course for you. It may have been something that took a lot of tenacity. It may have been something that stressed your abilities making you stronger and wiser along the way. Your failure sure sounds like a win.

I mentioned earlier that I fail every day. Some days, I want I work harder than other days and I fail to meet my own expectations. Some days, I want to relax and just listen to hifi and instead hit the phones and start scheduling appointments looking for new business. I know after a long day, my hifi will be there waiting for me as a nice reward to a productive day.

Besides, I wouldn't have the hifi if it wasn't for all the hard work I put in to afford it.

Have you ever wondered why and how winners win? Over the years, I have worked with a lot of winners. I have worked with Mr. Universe. I have worked with movie stars. I have worked with world-renowned musicians and even top-tier CEOs and they all say the same thing. It takes years and years of trial and error, wins and losses, successes and failures to get where they're at. Nobody wins without a fail. So what is a winner's mentality?

Watch a skateboard video sometime if you want to see what a winner's mentality REALLY looks like. The skateboarder has this goal of completing a seemingly impossible jump. They get a running start and make the first attempt and miss. They fall and scrape their arms. Now bloody, they try again, this time scraping their knees. Even more bloody, they try again. Fail. They try again. Fail. Fifteen or twenty times later, they finally land the trick. In the meantime, have they broke two skateboards, broke a finger, bleeding from their arm and their leg. They ruined their shoes and believe me, I am confident they are in pain. But, this feat was something that they had to try over and over until they landed it and when you watch the footage of the skateboarder completing the jump, all you see is the attempt they landed. This is very much like the people in life that tell me that I'm lucky for being where I'm at in life and no idea of the struggles it took to get where I'm at today.

Think about this with your business. Are you doing what is necessary to accomplish your goals? Have you gone bankrupt yet? I have and have zero regrets. Have you tried every possible outcome and still can't figure it out? Have you tried to the point where you're homeless living in your car? I have... twice. The point is, if you want something in life, YOU have to get it. It absolutely will not come to you. YOU have to go out there and do what is necessary to get it.

I ask myself all the time WHY I strive for so much in life, often times missing out on the fun and enjoyable things in life. Why have I sacrificed so much? Why didn't I just get a steady job and take the easy way out? Why do I work on holidays? Why do I work for hours and hours at a time and forget to eat? Why have I sold everything I own in order to take a risk and invest into an idea that isn't a sure thing? Honestly, I don't know.

I think about my childhood and the things I endured and wondered how I got through it. And so many people over the years have told me the past is in the past. The reality is, there is so much damage, I carry it with me every day. Every holiday I lose my will to live. I wait and wait hoping I get a call from somebody in my family and nothing. It's heartbreaking. It's like they all just forgot about me. For years, I have tried reaching out and those people want nothing to do with me, or many other people in the family.

When I met my wife, I was living in my car. The family I have today is my wife's family and they are incredible to me. They have giving me that element I have been missing my entire life. But there's still this feeling that I'm orphan waiting for my real family to come around and tell me they miss me. But every year at my birthday and Christmas, they don't.

The point of me telling you all of this is because as we continue to find success, we look for purpose

ACCOUNTABILITY

and winners need a sense of purpose. Winners strive for something bigger than them. They strive for accomplishment. They strive for excellence. They strive for acceptance. Winners channel into a missing element in their life or mind and overcome the challenge with a greatness that complacency incapable of.

ACCOUNTABILITY

Time Management

Time management is such an important aspect to your success that I wrote an entire book on it. The *4-Hour Work Day* has been a massive success selling copies all over the world. To date, it's my best selling book. Your success starts with just knowing how much you can fit into one day and still live a healthy life and have a quality work life and home life balance.

This entire chapter will stem from your good and bad habits. Do you like showing up early or are you always the last one into the meeting? Years ago, I used to sell cars and if you were the last one into the meeting, you better show up with donuts. If you didn't

ACCOUNTABILITY

shave before work, then you weren't ready to come to work and were usually sent home for the day. Things sure have changed in the work world from when I was spitting piss and vinegar. Today, not very many people have the work ethic that I would expect from them. A lot of my clients think I'm an asshole because I push them to be better. I KNOW they can do better and it's such a disappointment to see them making excuses for themselves. We will talk about excuses shortly. But, if you're late, it's because you're making excuses for yourself or don't respect the person you're meeting. There is zero excuse for punctuality issues.

The argument is, well I got a flat tire. Then plan for it. Be early. Or, there was traffic. C'mon, there's traffic every day. Plan for it. Get up earlier. But I don't get enough sleep already. Then go to bed earlier. You surely had enough time to watch the football game or watch your favourite show before bed.

ACCOUNTABILITY

Years ago, my wife and I threw our TV away. We have no television in our home. We did this for a lot of reasons. I assure you, we're never late anywhere. I have meetings with clients every single day. Usually, they are back to back. One at 11a, another at 1p and the final meeting at 3p. I will schedule my meetings near each other and I know my trip to the first meeting is about a half hour from my house. You may think I am crazy, but I will leave the house around 9a for my 11a meeting. Why is this? For one, I'm early.

I don't sit there like a goob in front their business waiting for them. That's rude. I will find a Starbucks and get work done. Whether it's editing client content or working on their website or even just returning emails. If I have nothing to do, I can work on my books or sometimes just sit and think and listen to music on my headphones. The bottom line is, I am ready to work when 11a comes around. I have looked over the client's wants and needs and know how I will help them before I even show up.

So, let's talk excuses. What happens if there's traffic? Well, I'm early so that doesn't matter. What if I get a flat tire or pulled over or just life happens? I was planning on being early and now I'm right on time. When you're on time, you spend less time stressing whether you will make it on time. That negative energy passes onto your client and that detriment passes doubt onto your client. Are you killing deals or having a low close ratio? Maybe you're just not ready to work.

There are so many times that I will be sitting at Starbucks getting work done and nature calls and I can comfortably take care of business without stressing if I am going to be late. Once, I was eating breakfast and spilled it all over my shirt. I had enough time to run home and change and still make it to my meeting and give them the service they deserve.

So, how do we better manage our time? We start by focusing on what's important first. If you have tasks that need done now that will take a considerable amount of time, get those done first. Then the less time sensitive ones can go next and the easy shit done last. Most people focus on the easy shit first and never make it to getting the important stuff done. Then they end up with all this shit that needs completed and don't have time to get any of it done.

I see so many small business owners doing things to look busy and not getting anything done. Instead, if they focused on the important shit, they could be busy and could actually be making progress.

ACCOUNTABILITY

Instead, they continue with their bad habits. Break these bad habits before they break you.

Wake up in the morning and have your task list and get shit done. If there are things in there that you don't need to do, don't do them. Family always comes first. Do not put your business first. Your clients and banks do not care about you and your kids. So why would you care about them? If your day starts with taking the kids to school, then get them off to school and make sure they are happy and healthy and ready for a productive day like yourself.

Show Up

Half of winning is just showing up. Do you have any idea how many business owners schedule meetings with me and either don't show up and cancel or reschedule for a later date? It's alarming. It's very sad and concerning but the way I look at it, it's their business. Maybe they are busy. Maybe something came up. The bottom line is, if they had a meeting with the President, I highly doubt they would reschedule the meeting. Make sense? Either they don't respect me or they don't respect their business. Or both.

I wake up some mornings and I just feel like shit. I don't want to go anywhere. I look at my calendar and think, I don't want to go to these meetings today. I think we all do this from time to time. I'll get up, grab a bite, hop in the shower and head out the door. I usually get to my meeting early and work from the car or from Starbucks or whatever and often times, I feel better. I'm ready to work. I wonder how many of those canceled appointments have the same thing happen but don't take the necessary steps. They cancel their meeting with me and an hour later, they are sitting there in their office or home wondering what they can do to improve their business.

Maybe they wanted to come to the meeting but didn't have the money to spend with me and didn't want the embarrassment of telling me they can't afford me. It makes sense. But money is just money. Money isn't anything. Once, I make them more valuable, more money will show up for them. If you're not sure what I am talking about, my book *Cash is Trash: Winning at the Game of Money* talks about all about it.

A lot of times, these clients that don't have the capital up front to work with me, I will put them on a payment plan and by the time their final payments are due, they are much more productive and profitable. So in reality, it doesn't cost them anything at all. The issue isn't that they don't have money or the drive or passion to build their business. The issue is they are giving up on themselves before they even give themselves the opportunity to win. You cannot win if you don't show up.

There was one week, I had 5 clients all tell me their father died. Either, that was a very unfortunate coincidence, or more and more small business

ACCOUNTABILITY

owners are making terrible excuses for themselves. Either way, only 1 or 2 of those clients I ended up rescheduling with and I no longer work with any of them to date. These excuses people make for themselves ultimately kill their business.

There was a time when an excuse almost killed the career of Will Smith. Will had just released his music album and went Platinum but was still broke. The reason for this is an entirely different book altogether as the record industry is not what most people think it is. His girlfriend at the time told him to talk to Arsenio to ask for help. He was invited to a party hosted by Quincy Jones and a group of other top industry executives to pitch a show called Fresh Prince. They offered him an audition and he asked for a couple weeks to prepare. They, in a kind way told him he had 10 minutes. He auditioned and nailed it. Had he waited, they would have had to get the lawyers and casting directors and show producers all back into the same room which is never an easy feat, leaving the roll open to another actor. The irony of this story was that he had to take the bus to meet with Arsenio. Had he just stayed home, he very well could be another forgotten name in show business. The way he says it, there is no worse feeling than being famous and riding the bus.

Because he showed up, he won. Another case is P!NK, when she met with L.A. Reid. She met with him in his car outside his office and handed him her demo. He was on the phone with a client and popped in the CD, listening while still on the phone leaving her standing there outside his car. She speaks up asking if he was going to listen or just keep talking. Apparently he didn't take offence to her demeanour because we know where her career has taken her.

ACCOUNTABILITY

The point is, both of these people showed up and took control. Half of winning is JUST SHOWING UP.

These clients that don't show up to these meetings with me, I don't know where they would be now. My ego isn't so big that I think they won't be successful me without me, but I do know human behaviour. If they miss the appointment with me, what other appointments are they missing? If they aren't paying the invoice on time with me, what other invoices aren't they paying? At what point are they no longer doing themselves any favours? At what point are they causing more harm than good by just letting opportunities slip by?

A Better You

We can all be better one way or another. Anybody who thinks otherwise is fighting a losing battle. When I got into the car business many years ago selling cars, the first thing I was taught was to stay green. In pretty much any sales industry, somebody who is just getting into an industry is called a 'green pea' and the advice given to me was to stay green, meaning to always be learning.

When you're just starting out as a 'green pea', you're in the learning phase. The issue with many sales industries is that egos get in the way and people start to think their shit doesn't stink. Those are the ones that get spun out first and forget how to ground themselves and usually end up having to fight the hardest to meet expectations. They will have good sales one month and get cocky again then the following month go back to being at the bottom of board. These are the folks that have zero consistency and usually either burn out or think the grass is greener elsewhere and jump dealership to dealership. Staying green allows you to consistently grow and become better through experience. You will win some months and lose other months but you're staying in your lane and growing a little at a time. Your ebbs and flows become more balance the more you learn and the longer you stay with it.

Everyday when you get up, set goals for yourself. Whether it's sales goals or personal goals. Always find ways to make yourself better. When I was in the mortgage business, I was always #1 in the company not because I was any better than anybody else, but because I set higher expectations for myself and went the extra mile. I have talked about this in many of my other books. I would arrive at work a few minutes early each day and would look at where the top performer was for the day and break their numbers into how many hours they were on shift. I would then double that number and break that into what I needed to accomplish per minute. If I fell short, I was still always better than whoever was in the top spot. It wasn't my ego I was fuelling, though it did feel good to win. I wanted the month-end bonuses they offered to the top performer each month. Whichever sales person was #1 would end up getting something like $2000 extra on their check at the end of month. Every month I worked for that company, I would get my bonus.

It wasn't that I was any better than anybody else. I truly believe we're all given the same gifts. I think we all just need to apply ourselves. I am sure you have heard the saying, "do what everybody else isn't doing." I expect you to do just that. When I wanted to be a professional guitarist or at the time, a rock star, I would practice my guitar nine hours each day. I was 15 years old. Here I am now 40 years old and no longer touring or have the aspirations of stage performing, but at home on my couch, I am still a better guitarist than the average player out there. Why? Because I put the time in to get there. I still write records and produce music for TV and movies. People tell me they heard my music on the Weather Channel or at a Fireworks show or wherever. And, I get my royalty checks deposited into my bank account each month.

ACCOUNTABILITY

I also write books. Some would say I write a lot of books. But, what is a lot of books? I think I have written something like 14 or 15 books now. I have in no way met my expectations for myself, therefore I will continue to write more and more books. These books motivate and inspire people all over the world and help them become better in their craft. Is my work done? No, I still have a lot to teach the world as I myself, continue to learn and figure things out. Yet, people tell me all the time that they could never write a book. They are probably right because they are too busy telling themselves it's too hard and spending that precious time watching television instead. We only get out of life what we put into life.

I have talked in many of my books about what money is and how it affects our life. Money is nothing more than the exchange of value for value. You have something of value trading for something else of value. If you become more valuable to people, you will in turn make more money. Whether it's getting a job and becoming more valuable to the employer or building a business and becoming more valuable to your industry, you will only get out what you put in.

So, what does being better mean? Put in the effort. Quit working so hard and start working smarter. They say that practice makes perfect but if you're practicing the wrong way, you're only going to get better at doing it wrong. If you're setting bad habits for yourself and you continue to practice those bad habits, those habits will be harder and harder to break. There's a saying, you cannot teach an old dog new tricks. I call bullshit. I see people every day, young and old, creating change in their life and becoming better. The question you have to ask yourself is, how bad do you want it and what are you willing to do to get it?

ACCOUNTABILITY

Are you willing to do things that take you from your comfort zone in order to win? What are you willing to risk? What does winning look like for you? Do you want to win or are you comfortable losing? Most people are comfortable losing and are afraid of the unknown of what winning looks like. Therefore, they choose comfort and choose their fate only wishing that something, someday will change for them. It's a sad reality.

Quit Making Excuses

Want to throw your life away? Then keep making excuses for yourself. Let's go over some of the best excuses I have heard recently.

Oh I could never do that. You're absolutely right. You could never do that IF you don't apply yourself. The problem here is the root of the statement. If you use fail words in your thinking, you will always fail. In this statement, the root is 'never'. By saying 'never', you immediately shut out the possibility of success or achievement. As an example, people tell me all the time they would love to write a book but could never do it. Why? Why can't you do it? Because you're lazy? Because you have a family to feed? Because you have a busy job? A lot of my writing happens in the car. I am sitting in my car right now as I write this waiting to head into a client meeting. I found time to write. A lot of times, I will be in traffic with my notepad open on my phone and using dictation software speaking my thoughts into my phone and using that to write my books. Let's get into our next excuse.

I don't have time. You would be surprised to know what you actually have and don't have time for. Do you watch TV? Well, then you have time. Why do I keep pointing blame at television? Because it's a time suck. Because a half hour or hour of television takes up a lot more of your life than you think. **But TV relaxes me before bed.** So would writing down your thoughts and your accomplishments. Have you ever wondered why there aren't Lamborghini or Bentley commercials on television? The answer might shock you. The answer is also quite simple. The people who buy and own Lamborghinis and Bentleys don't watch much television. It's not that they don't have time to watch TV, they just focus their energy on things that bring value and quality to their life. Like I said before, if you prioritise your time and focus on things that bring you value, then you are able to give the world more of you, making you more valuable to others.

I can't afford it. Oh this one gets me every time. I learned this one from one of Robert Kiyosaki's books. What I love so much about books is, you learn from the wisdom of others without taking decades of your life making the same mistakes. This is why I write so many books. I know that when I am gone, my wisdom will still be here helping others for generations to come. So, our excuse... I can't afford it. For one, our root of the excuse is 'can't'. By implying you can't do something, you immediately throw the idea of possibility out the window. Instead, maybe ask "how can I afford it?" At that point, you create the idea of what it will take to accomplish the goal and if you still feel that it doesn't make sense, then you have a real reason as to why you don't want to move forward.

I have always wanted to buy a Bentley but the thing that keeps coming back to me is a) the maintenance and b) putting a target on my back every time I go somewhere. Can I afford the car? Technically, yes. Do I want to spend my money on the car? Not really. Maybe someday when I have money to throw away, sure. But right now, I am just going to drive my Mercedes. It gets the job done. I have given considerable thought to Bentley ownership and the factor that scares me the most is sitting in traffic and being carjacked or even worse, my wife being carjacked. Living in the big city, nice cars and people wearing nice jewellery and being robbed in traffic for my watch just doesn't sound like fun.

You're just lucky. This one I have heard many times in my life. Let me tell you, there is no luck in my life. There has never been a 'right place at the right time'. Every single thing I have, even my wife, was earned the hard way. Here's a funny story about my wife and I.

I met her on a dating site many many years ago, way before there were dating apps. I must have emailed her a dozen times before she responded. She says the only reason she responded was because she was bored and I truly believe that. She was 23 and enjoying life and I was 30 looking for a wife. Two completely different ideals in life at the time. The irony is, once we met, we never left each other's side. We have always been there for each other. I was living in my car after losing my motorcycle shops. She was living at home with her folks. Pretty much everything I've built today, her and I did together.

In my 25 years as an entrepreneur, I have built probably 50 businesses. From selling Ferrari parts and motorcycle helmets to shooting movies and producing music to writing books and even attempting to build a TV network, we did it together. I even worked with Google for a while building an entrepreneur-based search engine. I've done it all. There is been no luck.

There's a saying successful people will tell you. It took 20 years to be an overnight success. There are a few circumstances where people hit it big, but even then, there was trials and lessons to be learned. The guy that wins $100 million in the lottery, that isn't a blessing. That is a curse. This guy has no idea how to manage that kind of money. Family will come out of the woodwork, IRS will have a fun time with them, he will want to cover his depression with spending sprees which will only fuel deeper depression. Nothing is free in life and there is no such thing as luck. There is only investment. You must invest and the more you invest in yourself, the more you will get in the long run.

    I watched a video the other night about an old man in Ecuador who sold Coconuts on the street corner. I think they called him The Coconut Man. He said he has no money and no home but is happy because that's all he has. Without happiness, we have nothing. Was he lucky to be alive? We all deserve to enjoy our life, long or short. This charity group came up and gave him money and a home and a future. Was it luck? I don't think so. He earned that. Through the joy and love he gave others, his sacrifices in life gave others the inspiration they needed to better their lives and in turn, the charity rewarded him. There was no luck there. Just the investment in himself rewarded by the investment of others.

It's too hard. Nothing in life is easy. Tell me one thing in life that is easy. Writing books? Though it has come pretty natural to me, I have had to take the time to master my craft and invest in myself. I was never good in school. I didn't come from a family of scholars. I was an abused kid with parents which neither went to college. So, how did it happen? How did I start writing books? One day, I had a dream that had a beginning, a middle and an end I wanted to capture it. I spent weeks writing, and telling the story of this dream. Now, all these years later, people still enjoy my book *Searching for Sara*.

I enjoy writing books. I enjoy story telling. I enjoy inspiring and motivating people through my experiences. You're probably reading this and wondering why my grammar sucks and why I don't use proper comma placement, that's because I'm uneducated. It's not an excuse. My work is an extension of me. I can use editors but choose not to. There's a ton of software programs out there that could polish my writing, but I feel it would lose the edge and rawness of my writing. However, I am wise. I have learned everything I know from reading and trial and error and my gift to the world is the wisdom I can bring others.

Was learning the guitar hard when I was kid? I didn't want to play the songs the other kids were playing. Kids have been playing the same shit for generations. You can only hear and play Iron Man so many times. Instead, I put on my inspiration... Joe

Satriani. Growing up I wanted to be just like this man. He got me through those hard times at home. The only thing I had growing up was my guitar. I've never had the support of family or friends. I was always alone. Listen to a lot of my early music, I am always mentioning sitting alone with my guitar.

Picking the guitar up at age 14 and starting to learn Satriani music at 15, yes it was hard. It's some of the most technically advanced guitar playing on the planet. But I took the time to listen to each note, finding them on the fretboard and mimicking the sounds creating and replicating his music. Around age 23 or 24, I went on tour playing a mix of my music and Satriani music every night on stage. By 30, I had developed a style of writing music very much like Satriani. And by 40, after meeting Joe many times and working with his team and producer, the music Joe releases today sounds like music I released a year ago. It's happened multiple times now. I have spoken with lawyers. I have broken his music down to see how much it sounds like mine and I have come to the conclusion that either he's using the same software tools to help his writing process or he's getting lazy and using the inspiration of other guitarist's structure to release his music. Either way, it's been hard to grasp.

The idea of giving up because something is hard only hurts where life will take you. With my ventures over the years, they have all been hard. There are trials. There are times I don't know what moves to make. There are times, I'm not sure where life is taking me. I just stay the course and focus on what I want to achieve. I continue to set new goals for myself and let life happen. We really have little control over where life takes us, but God has a plan. The universe has a plan. Something has something in

ACCOUNTABILITY

store for us. We just need to follow our intuition and use our talents and skills to see where life is taking us. But making excuses and leaning on laziness is the last thing you want to do IF you want to be successful.

And sitting here waiting for my 11a to show up, she's late. I'm sure she has a great excuse. Winners will win. Losers will make excuses.

Setting Goals

Goal setting is imperative to your success. Without setting proper goals, you don't have a road map guiding you to where you want to go. Think of setting goals like a GPS for your success. In fact, think of GPS as Goal > Productivity > Success.

If you wanted to go to Disneyland for instance, you don't just get into the car and drive in a random direction and hope to arrive at your destination. You first know where you want to go. Then, you map out a plan to get there, whether that be getting onto the highway or taking a plane. Then, you know once you've made it to Los Angeles, to follow the appropriate roads to successful arrive at Disneyland. Success is no different.

Tony Robbins talks a lot about goal setting and says to think of your destination in reverse if you want to successfully meet your goals. For instance, if you want to save $10,000 next year and you randomly start putting $5 bills into a drawer, chances are you will fall short. Instead, think about breaking your $10,000 into months, weeks, and days. Earlier I talked about how I become #1 in sales when I did mortgages, I did the same thing. I broke my day into hours and minutes and had expectations for myself. Do the same thing with your goals.

If you want to save $10,000 in a year, you know that you need to put away $27.40 per day. If you are used to spending $30 on lunch everyday at work, maybe bring a sandwich from home instead. You can always skip your Starbucks trips and make coffee at home. Find a shorter route to work so you use less fuel. Watch less television and cancel your TV subscriptions. Quit shopping at Amazon before falling asleep at night. Impulse buys really take a lot of our money. Paying off credit cards so you have more liquid cash and reducing the amount you spend on interest is a great way to reduce monthly spending. Your goal of saving $10,000 really comes easy when you build the roadmap to get there.

We all have goals closing out one year and going into another. Yet, every year we continue to make resolutions for ourselves. It's not that we aren't motivated to meet our goals, I think it's just how we execute those goals. 41% of Americans make a New Year's Resolution. And, by year end, only 9% of them have kept their goal. This stems from creating good and bad habits and setting realistic goals with a plan to execute that goal.

Remember GPS, Goal > Productivity > Success. To be successful, you must set your goal. Then, execute the goal with productivity and make sure to follow through. Don't half ass it. It's always easier and more efficient to get it done right the first time than having to do it twice. And then finally, once you have done what was necessary, mark it off your list and go onto the next goal…Success!

ACCOUNTABILITY

The Extra Mile

We have all heard of going the extra mile. What does that mean? I think people mistake going the extra mile as doing a lot or doing more than what is asked of them. Sometimes, a lot of times, that's just doing too much and actually can cause detriment in your business and your relationships. Everybody knows that posting on social media is important to the success of your business because it's a great tool to communicate your message to your audience. But imagine posting something every 2 minutes. Before long, your audience is no longer interested in your message. In a sense, you went the extra mile, but in the wrong context.

Another way we do this wrong is by getting into our own way. I see a lot of clients that step on their own feet and either limit their success or impair their success. They want to look and feel busy in order to fuel their egos, but they aren't doing anything to help their business or brand. They just put out shit products or advertising or schedule useless meetings and get nothing done. We see this a lot with small business owners.

I was told once that there is no rhyme or reason why a small business stays small or why an entrepreneur can't get their business off the ground and that the ones that do, are the lucky ones. I call bullshit. If a small business owner wants to stay small, they typically will. And if a small business owner wants to grow, they have to do what is necessary to get there, ie: the shit I talk about in this book.

I choose to keep my business tight. I'm the type of person that doesn't like red tape and nonsense. I want to keep to myself and live my life and work with the people I want to work with. And if there is a client that is more trouble than they are worth, I typically get rid of them and move on with my life. It is very important that we don't 'go the extra mile' and sell ourselves short. A client that is a pain in the ass at the beginning of the working relationship, only becomes a bigger pain in the ass as time goes on. Let those people work with somebody else.

So, what does going the extra mile mean? It means to do good work. Provide quality. Provide value. When you leave that project, you should feel good about it. You should feel like you did the client or customer right. Invest in yourself. Invest in your client or customer. Shake their hand. Remember their name. Build the relationship and make sure they are complimenting your goals and what you want your client base to look like.

If your client base is all a bunch of junk businesses, it will be hard for you to find better clients as shit usually gravitates toward shit. If you are a reputable business and do good work, typically you will gravitate toward better clients and get quality referrals in return. Always remember that you don't have to work with every client. I let clients go all the time. That is part of me going the extra mile. By eliminating the junk clients, I can provide more value and better assist my quality clients. I know that if one of my clients calls on a Saturday or outside of business hours, it's usually going to be a good conversation and not a bad one.

Better educate yourself in your field and the field of your client base. It's important for your rapport if you know a little more about what your clients do for a living. This builds a bond or friendships out of your clients. This leads to future referrals and repeat business. It also leads to positive reviews online. Reviews are great for your business. Once you get those reviews, don't be afraid to reach out and thank them for their review. Again, another simple way of going the extra mile.

Setting Expectations

Setting expectations is very important to your success. Whether we're talking about your business, your job, your relationships or whatever, you absolutely should have expectations. When you start your day, you have expectations as to where your day will go, right? When I get up, I know that I need to take a shit that day. I know that I need to find a deal, or at the least find some leads. I know that I need to take my dog for a walk and kiss my wife before walking out the door. I know that I need to be respectful of my life and not die. My wife has expectations for me as well. She expects me to be faithful and come home and enjoy our evening and continue life together.

I dated a girl once that kept telling me I shouldn't have expectations. She said I should just enjoy the moment and whatever happens, happens. I am sure you all have heard this before and I am sure there is a little truth to this in terms of enjoying the moment. We all need to stop and smell the roses every once in a while. And life will happen whether we're in the equation or not. After we're gone, the sun will rise the next day and life will go on. However, we must set expectations for ourselves. And, we must have expectations in others.

Imagine running a business and your employee tells you not to have expectations and whatever happens, happens. They probably won't work there long. Imagine saying that to your wife. You walk out the door and kiss your wife goodbye and she says be careful and drive safe and you tell her, "whatever happens, happens." That's a shitty feeling to start a day with. Expectations are important for our day to day life.

I look at business like a marriage. When I bring on a new client, we both have high expectations for each other. They are hiring me to help them with a problem and at the same time, I am hiring them to help me with a problem. Remember, value = value. They want me to help them grow their business. And, I want them to help me grow mine. They give me money and I give them services. It's a win win for everybody, IF expectations are set up front.

At your initial sit-down with your potential client, sometimes you need to have that heart to heart with them. You need to tell them that if we move forward, they need to meet their obligations or it's no deal. Why is this so important if they are the one hiring you? Imagine you sitting there and explaining what you do and they take an interest and it's time to move the deal forward. You send over the invoice and wait. Two days turns into a week into a month and nothing happens. You reach out and now it's not a deal. They changed their mind. You never set proper expectations from the beginning. Instead, you send the invoice and ask them when it will be paid. If they tell you tonight and three days later, they are still heehawing about making payment, one of two things happened. Either, you didn't sell yourself well enough or you just encountered a shit client. Reach back out and ask them why the reluctancy? If they express concerns or have questions, you can typically sort those out. But, if they are saying paying will be tonight and it's still not there in two days, kill the deal and move on.

I have run into this many times in my career and I am always the one at fault right? I'll have a client pull this nonsense and then I block them on social media and on my phone and move on with life and two or more years later, I will run into them again forgetting the situation and they will tell me they need my services. The process starts all over again and then I will remember what happened and again, no payment of invoice. These people just bumble through life kicking tires and wasting people's time. Yet, as you continue to grow, you will start to see all those shitty clients you let go all working together in a little miserable group hating your guts because you're so mean and rude and your success is just luck.

ACCOUNTABILITY

We are who we surround ourselves with. Some call it the circle of seven. Some call it a sphere of influence. Whatever you want to call it, if you surround yourself with a bunch of people with bad habits, you will find yourself making those same bad habits. Have expectations for your friends. Have expectations for yourself. Hold you and your friends to a higher regard.

Should you hold all of your friends to the same regard? I don't think so. I have 3 tiers of friends as I do my clients. I have the A group, B group and C group. My A group of friends are much like my A group of clients. And, at any point they can fall into the B or C group as I have expectations for them. My A group are the people I will answer the phone for regardless of day or time and I am always happy to hear from them. The B group, I will call back if I am in the middle of something. And the C group, I don't call unless there's a reason to call. What constitutes the A group? Respect.

If I have a friend or client in the A group and I need something or want to check in to say hi and they don't answer and I call again the next day and they don't answer and 3 days later, there's no call or text back, immediately into the B group they go. If I see them in public, I have no will ill toward them. I just figured they were busy and needed space, so I gave it to them. And the C group are just more of acquaintances that we can trust to get the job done but we don't need to speak unless there's something on the table.

It is very important that you set expectations for yourself and treat everybody with the care and respect that you would expect from yourself.

ACCOUNTABILITY

Success Isn't Luck

The idea the success is luck is ludicrous. There are millions upon millions of people out there striving toward something. They have wants and desires and many of them never meet the goals they set for themselves. This isn't because they aren't smarter than anybody else and it's also not because they aren't working toward it or for it. I truly believe the reason why most people don't meet the goals they set for themselves is because they don't focus their energy in the right areas.

If you get into a relationship and the relationship doesn't work out, I wouldn't say that only lucky people have successful relationships.

Successful relationships happen from the investment in the relationship. If both parties aren't willing to do what it takes to make that relationship work, then how could they expect the relationship to get them where they want it to? Success is no different.

People tell me all the time that they are trying everything to get their business to work and nothing works. Sometimes, most times, people want to do what is comfortable to them and not what the project demands. As a business consultant, many of my clients think I am picking on them because I point out where they can improve. If they give me excuses, I tell them that excuses don't work with me.

There's a meme I saw quite some time ago that explains success very clearly. The photo shows the tip of an iceberg. This is what the public sees when they think of success. But the iceberg's mass is under water. That mass in success are the trials, failures, late nights, missed meals, failed relationships, bad reviews, lost deals, refunds, missed opportunities and so on. Most people aren't successful NOT because they aren't lucky. They just don't want to invest what is necessary in order to win.

Another mistake a lot of entrepreneurs make is winning once and thinking they made it to the finish line. Entrepreneurship is a marathon. There is no winner. Ever. You win when you die and you leave a legacy behind. And I'm not talking about a legacy of wealth. I have said it before and I will say it again. Nobody cares what kind of shoes you're wearing when you die. All they care about is what kind of person you were. Were you an asshole? Or, were you compassionate and loving and intelligent and generous? Were you a good mother or father or brother or sister? Were you a good community member? Did you contribute to the book of knowledge? Where are you leaving your name and what does your name say about you?

Let's also get into the definition of success. Success is the accomplishment of aim or purpose, meaning if you accomplished your goal, you were successful. I think too many people, including myself turn to inspiration from social media and magazines to define success. We want the nice cars and watches and clothes and home and even our spouse needs to look and act a certain way. We as a society, get too wrapped up in looking a certain way that we never truly find success. Are you the person you wanted to be? Are you holding yourself to the standard you set for yourself? Are you setting your bar too high, or right where you should be?

Dream Big

If you want to be successful in business, look at what everybody else is doing and do the exact opposite, but make sure that it's providing more value to the client, you're providing a better-quality product and that you're 100% ethical.

Some time ago, I told a friend of mine that someday I wanted my name on an arena (Jon Robert Quinn Arena). He laughed at me and then never spoke to me again. Sometime later, I heard that he thought I was so arrogant that he could no longer be friends with me. Fast forward a few years and he's a bartender and I'm a national talk show host selling books all over the world. My dream doesn't seem so far-fetched anymore because I'm closer to my goal. Maybe a month ago, I sent a text to an investor friend of mine saying I wanted to build skyscrapers and he replied with a list of everything I needed to do. From that moment, I got to work. My focuses changed and I no longer want to build skyscrapers, but I learned a wealth of knowledge along the way to that realisation.

When you look at your business and gauge where you've been and where you're going, does it all make sense? Set high goals and work toward them every single day. Business is a practice. There are a million ways to be successful. You just need to find a formula that works for you. I get what I need to get done when it needs done. But, if you're more trouble that you're worth, I'll move on.

Have you built a business or built a job? Pay attention to your surroundings. The answers are right in front of you. Business is like jump rope in elementary school. You're always waiting for that perfect time to jump in, but the perfect time may have already come and gone. If you're going to win, you've got to go all in.

I see all these posts of people with $20k watches and Bentleys and stacks of money and what does it all mean? Is this what motivates you? Are you working hard or working smart and are you working for right reasons? Are you trying to BE successful or LOOK successful? Are you trying to enrich your life and those around you or create an imaginary world to get attention? There's nothing wrong with being successful and having dreams, I just find it hard to believe that there are so many people with stacks of cash when they are all using the same pictures on social media.

ACCOUNTABILITY

What are you doing differently today that you didn't try yesterday? Your success will come from your burning desire to succeed. Nothing should ever stop you from succeeding. We all have an excuse and a reason why we can't do something, however when we have no other choice, we always seem to make it work.

Success isn't all about big spending. It's about spending on the right things. Every day, I see people who once had a lot of money end up with no money. When your success starts, the question shouldn't be what can you buy, it should be what shouldn't you buy. The rich buy things that make them money. The poor buy things that cost them money. Which one are you?

Today, see things as challenges and tackle them all one by one. As the day closes, you will have a sense of achievement that you can take into the following day. Find the positive in everything. Do this and nothing can break you.

Fridays are good days. Not only because it leads to the weekend, Fridays allow us to analyse our behaviours of the week allowing us to correct our behaviours for the week ahead. Analysing and correcting our behaviours allows us to grow in ourselves making us stronger and more successful.

People think too much. In order to be big, you must do big. And in order to do big, you must think big. Often times, people who think they are big, aren't big. Therefore, you must do big to be big and leave the thinking to thinkers. The thinkers work for you and think someday they will be big but won't because they think too much. Don't like it? Do something about it. Often times, the people that read Think and Grow Rich don't do much, yet think they do. Do less thinking and more doing.

ACCOUNTABILITY

It's not what you know, it's who you know. Sitting behind your computer all day won't get you anywhere except maybe a hospital bed. You need to be networking with the RIGHT people and growing your brand.

ACCOUNTABILITY

Fear Will Cripple You

There are days when I wake up and don't want to go to work. I'm no different than anybody else. I get up and do what is necessary and call it a day when I close a deal or two. Regardless, the job gets done. I make the necessary calls, follow up on leads, send out emails, send out messages on social media, post ads on social media, record a show or two, complete post production and send to the station to air. I can get all of this done in a few short hours. You don't have to work 95 hours a week like our good ol' friend Grant Cardone.

However, you've got to be fearless otherwise you're fearful and being fearful will cripple you and your business. The business world is like a war zone. You'll be taken out by your opponent if you don't take them out first. You need to know your every move before you make it and make sure you are sure-footed about your approach to business. They say that if you're going to walk the ledge of a mountain with a steep cliff, to use a horse to do it and ride the horse. Sounds crazy, but the horse will never miss a step. Make sure your mind is ready for battle and be ready to take out your opponents.

So often I hear the words I can't or I'm tired. We are all tired and yes you can. You just choose not to. When I call a client and it goes to voicemail and the message says something like, "I can't make it to the phone", I know this client will be full of excuses. I know it sounds petty, but even using the word "can't" in your vocabulary has a dramatic effect on you and your business. Never use the word and furthermore, never make excuses for yourself. Just get the job done.

You have to remove yourself from your comfort zone if you want to grow. You will never ever grow if you're playing it safe. Winners take chances and you must do the same thing. It's so funny that every single time a client says they want to think about it, they talk themselves out of it and then I will run into them in two or three years and they are doing the same thing they were when we spoke years prior. Their lives are literally exactly the same. Then when they see where my life is, they tell me I'm lucky. It's not luck folks. I worked my ass off to get where I'm at.

The closer closes the deal from the moment the client takes the seat. The man who stalls or loses any control loses the deal. When you walk into a car dealership, the good sales guy knows he selling you a car from the moment he shakes your hand. The shitty sales guy would like to sell a car but would most rather sit back down in his chair and get back to the game on his phone. When you're in the mindset to win, you'll win every time. But, what happens if they don't qualify and the deal doesn't work out? You still won because your head was in the game and if you kept their info, you can follow back up in six months or whatever and try the deal again.

    Having the opportunity to meet Grant Cardone, a man worth $840,000,000 didn't happen on accident. I knew where he was going and when he would be there. I knew when his plane was landing, where it was landing and when he would arrive to the event. This is how prepared you should be during every business transaction. Imagine knowing your opponent so well that you knew what moves he was making before he made them. That's how you win. Going in blind sets you up for failure.

ACCOUNTABILITY

The only way to outperform your competition is to always find the advantage. The only way to do that is with wisdom. Well, since we all have the same time in the day, the best way to become smarter is to read. It sure beats having to learn from your own mistakes.

People are always trying to make us into someone they want us to be. Instead, be that person you want to be. NEVER GIVE UP. There is something special about a fighter. You fight to WIN. There are no winners without a FIGHT.

One of the most important parts of growth is knowing when to push hard and when to ease off. Doing too much causes you to lose focus and make mistakes. Doing too little allows you to focus on things that don't matter inhabiting failure. Never count your chickens before they hatch. What works today doesn't always work tomorrow so always be thinking about what's next.

ACCOUNTABILITY

Spend less time saving and more time creating money. More money won't solve your problems, but changing your thought process will. People are poor not because of how much money they make or how they spend their money, but because of mindset. Too many people say, "I can't afford it" instead of "how can I afford it?" One closes the opportunity, the other opens all possibilities.

Your value isn't determined by how much money you have but by how much money you can create. Why do 99% of small businesses fail in the first five years? Fear. The fear of failing will kill your business every time. Every small business owner knows it's vital to amp up advertising during the holidays. Businesses also want to see 100% ROI. Then why are most small business only spending $250 on marketing? IS THAT ALL YOUR BUSINESS IS WORTH? Wake up, you're going broke.

ACCOUNTABILITY

Conclusion

This book is about accountability and holding yourself accountable in order to win. Are you willing to do what it takes? Are you willing to stay up those late nights in order to meet your goals? Are you setting the right goals? Are you being honest with yourself? Are you making excuses for yourself?

I have a client I recently had to let go. She's a wonderful person, full of love and heart and brightens a room when she walks in. Her eyes are infectious. Her smile is warm and inviting. She has a very soothing way about her that makes it very easy to like her. What she doesn't have is confidence and it throws her entire product out the window.

She doubts herself and says she should get into a new line of work because it's just not working for her anymore. She gets depressed and spends her time making excuses. She wastes her valuable time on things that don't produce results. I have tried for several months to mentor her. She doesn't like the advice or critiques. She tells me she's been doing real estate for 20 years. The sad thing is, a lot has changed in 20 years and I know many real estate professionals that are doing quite well right now because their head is in the right space.

There have been times I would call her and she would be crying because she doesn't know how to pay her bills. But then has money to go to the casino and buy nonsense online. She invests heavily into her business with little to no result. She's a very smart woman that knows her craft and knows it well. So where is the missing link? Accountability.

ACCOUNTABILITY

She makes excuses for herself which throws all accountability out the window. If she sat down and just started making appointments and connecting with people on social media, she would have business. Instead, she watches television and waits for the phone to ring. If she's reading this book right now and knows I am referencing her and feels like I am picking on her, the problem still isn't me. I hold myself accountable every day.

There are days I don't want to get up for work. I do anyway. There are days I don't have money to do some of the fun things I want to do. I figure it out. There are days I don't know where I am going to find my next leads. It always works out because I make sure I do what is necessary. There was a time when I had to decide whether to spend my wedding anniversary at home with my wife or shoot scenes for a movie 3000 miles away. We celebrated early and I got the job done for the film. The point is, we are all human and we all make mistakes, but our success comes from our willingness to hold ourselves accountable.

Regarding the client I had to let go, she's a great lady. I would love to work with her again, someday. But, she really needs to work on herself. The saying goes, you can never make somebody happy if you're not happy with yourself. She needs to get out of her head, quit overthinking, focus on what she wants in life, step into some uncomfortable situations in order for her to grow and adapt, and hopefully by setting goals for herself and doing what it takes to accomplish those goals, her and I can work together more toward making her more valuable to her clients.

As for you... You've made it this far in this book. I hope you have learned a few things and can apply this into your life in order to see where it takes you. None of us have all the answers. None of us have a crystal ball. But, we do have a toolbox full of tools we have picked up along the way that help us overcome the challenges life gives us and by using these lessons and ideas in this book, you can accomplish the things you want in life.